Maximum Discipleship in the Church

A Church Leader's Guide for Building a Strategic Approach to Making Disciples

Randy Wolff

Copyright © 2017 by **Dr. Randy Wollf**

All rights reserved. No part of this publication may be reproduced, distributed, or transmitted in any form or by any means without prior written permission.

Dr. Randy Wollf
7600 Glover Road
Langley, BC, Canada
V2Y 1Y1
www.randywollf.com

Publisher's Note: This book is based on numerous conversations with church leaders, the perspectives of those who have written books on discipleship and my own observations as a leader in the church for the past 25 years.

Copy Editing: Ruth Engler at PaperLift Document Editing (www.PaperLift.com)
Cover Design: Calvin Hanson Creative (www.calvinhanson.com)

Maximum Discipleship in the Church: A Church Leader's Guide for Building a Strategic Approach to Making Disciples / Dr. Randy Wollf -- 1st ed.
Part of the MinistryLift Church Leadership Series (Book #1)
Print Edition ISBN 978-1979883931

Table of Contents

Introduction - Developing a Discipleship Approach in Your Church 5

Chapter 1 - Prayer Saturation 13

Chapter 2 - Growing Relationships 21

Chapter 3 - Growth Orientation 27

Chapter 4 - Personalized Approach 35

Chapter 5 - Missional Mindset in Your Church 39

Chapter 6 - Biblical and Engaging Preaching 51

Chapter 7 - Effective Group Training 59

Chapter 8 - Robust Small Groups 65

Chapter 9 - Supportive Accountability 75

Chapter 10 - Coaching/Mentoring 81

Chapter 11 - Spiritual Disciplines 95

Chapter 12 - Next Steps 107

Introduction

Developing a Discipleship Approach in Your Church

Church leaders often ask me, "How do we develop a discipleship strategy in our church?" To begin to answer this question, we need to define two important terms and address some other questions first.

What is Discipleship?

Discipleship is both relational and transformational. A disciple of Jesus is in a growing relationship with Jesus. Transformation occurs as the Holy Spirit renovates people's hearts. As a result, godly character qualities grow, and thoughts and actions become more God-honoring.

According to Dallas Willard, "Discipleship is the process of becoming who Jesus would be if he were you." This requires a close relationship (see John 15) that produces Christ-like fruit.

What is Disciple-making?

Disciple-making is helping people take next steps in their relationship with Jesus and obedience to Him.

In *Real-life Discipleship*, Jim Putnam suggests that there are five spiritual stages: 1) dead, 2) infant, 3) child, 4) young adult, and 5) parent. It is helpful to identify the stages in which people are located so that we can come alongside them and help them move toward the next stage. As we help people become more spiritually mature, we need to help them:

1. Grow in their relationship with God
2. Develop godly character qualities
3. Understand and live out God's calling on their lives
4. Develop strong relationships
5. Learn how to serve well on a team
6. Maximize their gifts and abilities in living out their calling.

How do Churches Position Themselves for Maximum Discipleship?

Based on numerous conversations with church leaders, the perspectives of those who have written books on discipleship and my own observations as a leader in the church for the past 25 years, I suggest that there are five layers of discipleship within the church: 1) church culture, 2) large group, 3) small group, 4) one-on-one, and 5) individual. As we strengthen each layer, we will position our churches for more effective disciple-making (which is the focus of this book).

Layer #1 - Church Culture

Obviously, we want our people to make disciples naturally as they go through their day. Five cultural factors facilitate this kind of continuous disciple-making:

1. **Prayer Saturation** - Prayer permeates disciple-making churches. How can we grow a culture of prayer – a culture in which God delights to work deeply in peoples' lives?

2. **Loving Christ-centered Community** - Discipleship occurs best in deep communities where people lovingly practice life-on-life discipleship. What can leaders do to develop this kind of intimacy?

3. **A Growth Orientation** - When everything in the church is geared toward helping people take next steps, growth becomes normative and expected. Discipleship can flourish in this kind of growth-oriented environment.

4. **A Personalized Approach** - Even though programs can provide a context in which discipleship can occur, we must strive to come alongside individuals and help them take next steps. This personalized approach is a requirement for in-depth discipleship.

5. **A Missional Mindset** - Without a strong desire to reach lost people, churches are unlikely to have the passion and motivation to devote a significant amount of time and energy to making disciples. A main goal of making disciples is so that we can make more disciples.

As a church facilitates growth in these five areas,

people will be much more inclined to be and make growing disciples of Jesus.

It may be helpful to view this church culture layer as the soil in which discipleship grows in a local church. As we strengthen these five cultural dimensions, we enrich the soil so that discipleship can flourish.

The next four layers of a church discipleship approach move from a global level (church-wide culture) to an individual level. As we move toward the inner layers, we are often able to make our discipleship much more personal and relevant to the individual. These layers provide the necessary structure to promote spiritual growth in the church (like a trellis does with a vine).

Layer #2 - Large Groups

Discipleship that occurs in our worship services and large group training events (e.g. a marriage-builder course) is vitally important. We need biblical teaching that inspires us to move forward in our Christian lives. We need practical training to equip us with knowledge and skills that build capacity in us to love God and others more deeply and serve Him (and others) more effectively.

Layer #3 - Small Groups

Small groups have immense potential for becoming loving Christ-centered communities on a mission to be and make growing disciples of Jesus. Robust small groups do four things well: 1) prayer, 2) outreach, 3) care, and 4) empowerment. When small groups are growing in these four areas, they will be in a stronger position to see people come to Christ and grow in him.

Layer #4 - One-on-one

Coaching/mentoring is a wonderful way to come alongside people in a highly personalized way and walk with them as they take steps in their personal growth. A coaching approach that moves beyond simply listening and asking good expanding questions (as important as these are) to lovingly calling people to action (and following up with supportive accountability) is a key discipleship strategy.

Layer #5 – Individual Spiritual Disciplines

We all recognize the importance of spiritual disciplines like prayer and meditating on Scripture. The purpose of spiritual disciplines is to help us live a life of spiritual discipline where we surrender every part of our lives to Him. As people grow in their capacity to live spiritually disciplined lives, they will live as vibrant disciples of Jesus who actively make disciples of others.

Let's return to the question I posed at the start: "How do we develop a discipleship strategy in our churches?" I suggest that we need to work diligently to strengthen each of these five layers while recognizing that the five cultural elements are foundational to the growth of the other elements. As we strengthen the large group, small group, one-on-one and individual layers, we look for ways to help people mature in Christ (i.e. moving people through Jim Putnam's spiritual stages mentioned above). To help us do this, we assess how people are doing in each of the six dimensions of discipleship (e.g. godly character) and then preach, teach, facilitate, and coach in ways that help people take next steps in the areas of greatest need.

How to Make the Best Use of this Book

In the next 11 chapters, we will look at each of these essential elements for making disciples in your church. I encourage you to read this book as a church leadership team. You can also get other leaders in the church to read the book, so that you're all on the same page. It would also be very helpful if you and your leadership team would do the online Church Discipleship Assessment (see access information at the end of this book). The assessment measures your church's current effectiveness in the 11 disciple-making areas. You will likely find that doing the assessment before reading the book will inform your reading and follow-up discussions.

In addition to reading the book and doing the assessment, take time to think through and discuss the questions at the end of each chapter. You can do this at your regular leadership meetings (e.g. staff meetings, board meetings, volunteer leader meetings) or at a larger leadership retreat dedicated to developing a church discipleship approach. My hope is, that in these prayerful discussions, you will sense what God would have you to do next in making disciples more effectively as a church.

If you would prefer to watch me talk about this content in video format or would like to supplement this material with other discipleship resources, you can go to the discipleship page on the MinistryLift website: www.ministrylift.ca/discipleship.

My prayer is that God would use this book to simulate thought and action toward even stronger disciple-making approaches in our churches.

Reflection/Discussion Questions

1. From your perspective, what is a disciple of Jesus?
2. What is discipleship?
3. What disciple-making approaches are working in your church?
4. What are the practical implications of Dallas Willard's definition of discipleship: "Discipleship is the process of becoming who Jesus would be if he were you?"
5. What are some of the discipleship emphases that would be important in each of Putnam's five stages (dead, infant, child, young adult, parent)?
6. Thinking about the six discipleship goals (help people grow in their relationship with God, develop godly character qualities, understand and live out God's calling on their lives, develop strong relationships, learn how to serve well on a team, and maximize their gifts and abilities in living out their calling), which ones are you currently doing well in your church?
7. If you were to choose one of the six discipleship goals to emphasize more, which one would you choose? How would you strengthen this area over the next year?
8. Thinking about the five layers of discipleship (church culture, large group, small group, one-on-one, individual), which layer is quite strong in your church? How might you strengthen one of the weaker layers?

9. What are some additional thoughts emerging from this chapter?

Chapter 1

Prayer Saturation

It's five years from now. Amazingly, your church has grown incredibly in prayer. People are setting aside time each day to pray. They're worshipping God throughout the day. You see life groups and ministry groups making prayer a central part of their group life. You see a church where God is doing amazing things as He responds to the prayers of His people.

Sound exciting? How do we realize this kind of vision? Here are several ways to strengthen prayer in your church:

Enlarge People's Vision for Prayer

How do we challenge people to grow deeper in prayer? Preaching and teaching on prayer definitely helps. In addition, here is an idea that can blow away people's conceptions about how God can respond to prayer today: tell people about some of the spiritual revivals that have happened over the past 300 years (for starters, search for *The Role of Prayer in Spiritual Awakening* video by Dr. J. Edwin Orr). Knowing how God has responded to concerted, extraordinary prayer in the recent past can inspire us to pray in focused and persistent ways today.

Equip People to Pray

Most Christians know how to ask God for stuff. Yet, do we truly practice thankfulness, confession, and adoration of God? Do we realize deep down that the goal is not just to pray for a set period each day (as good as that is), but to develop a lifestyle of prayer?

We can teach about prayer through sermons and workshops, but there is nothing quite like combining training with practice. One of the most powerful equipping times for my church leadership team was when we went on a two-day prayer retreat. We all read a book on prayer prior to the retreat, took in some training sessions during the retreat, and then spent time in prayer. It was powerful!

Build on What is Already Happening

Sometimes, we think that we need to create something new to stimulate more prayer in our churches. That may be helpful, but we should probably start with what is already in place.

For example, when I was co-chair of our church board, we extended our dedicated prayer times and incorporated prayer throughout our business discussions. This small change had considerable impact.

Small group Bible studies and ministry groups provide an excellent forum for strengthening prayer in your church. Inspire your leaders with a big vision for prayer. Train them and give them solid prayer resources. When leaders really pray, others will follow their example.

Incorporate Rallying Prayer Initiatives

Make the most of people's willingness to commit to something significant for a short period of time. For example, some churches will organize a day or week of prayer where people sign up to pray at different times.

...did 40 days of prayer during Lent
...couraged to pray for specific as-
...ach day. However, this particular
...xpectations. Even though it was a
...ers could have done more to keep
...going by keeping the prayer cam-
...of people's thinking.

...n challenged groups to pray for five un-
...ays a week for five weeks. These
...nitiatives get people praying and
...em develop a stronger habit of

...hnology and Social Media

...nternet allows us to share prayer
...e praying within seconds. Small
...ook groups, use apps that have
...WhatsApp or GroupMe), or cap-
...ng platforms to promote prayer

Grow a Vital Sunday Morning Prayer Ministry

When you have a vital Sunday morning prayer ministry, God will show up in people's lives in amazing ways.

For example, at South Langley Church, we often have an open mic sharing time during our worship services. One Sunday, a woman shared about how she had gone up for prayer (we have a post-service prayer ministry) a few weeks previously about her recent cancer diagnosis. After our prayer team prayed for her, the woman felt that God had healed her. Her doctor wasn't so sure. He tried to convince her that the first test was conclusive. Finally, after she pleaded with him, the doctor authorized another test. The new test result revealed that the woman was cancer-free.

You can imagine how the congregation responded to this obvious answer to prayer. As we see God work, we will be more likely to believe that He can do immeasurably more that we could ever ask or imagine.

Model and Encourage Interpersonal Prayer

Structured prayer times are important and necessary. Yet, we also want to encourage people to pray spontaneously with one another. The pastors at South Langley will periodically remind us to look for opportunities to pray for one another even as we visit with people after the service.

We can also encourage interpersonal prayer in our small groups. It could be as simple as inviting group members to call one another during the week or to send email/text prayers.

Encourage the Prayer Warriors

You probably already have people in your church who are extraordinary intercessors. Make sure that you thank them and appreciate them in appropriate ways. Supply them with prayer requests. If they are willing, let them share about their prayer practices and how God has worked through them. Your people will be inspired!

Be Bold in Taking Next Steps

Pastor Chris sensed that God wanted his church to have dedicated prayer groups praying every day of the week. He knew there would be opposition, so he tried to dismiss the growing conviction in his spirit. Finally, he realized that he had to obey the voice of the Lord. Within two months, they had 10 prayer groups that covered every day of the week!

Here's what Pastor Chris said about seven months into their church's prayer venture:

> Prayer has fundamentally changed the culture of the church. It has also stirred up a lot of spiritual warfare. I realized a month in when things started to get crazy and challenging that the reason was that when we decided to be a praying church, it was essentially a declaration of war on the Enemy.
>
> That has changed everything. It has also shifted how we look at everything. Prayer goes first and is what we rely on. We don't do anything unless we pray about it first. And when we pray, we wait on the Lord. It hasn't been easy to keep up the persistence, but the reward is that we are seeing breakthrough. When people pray together, they grow closer. The relationships are more real and the stuff we talk about is not superficial. Also, the Spirit shows us so much more about who we are when we constantly ask Him.
>
> An unfortunate result is that some people have left the church as a result of the shift to prayer. When God gave me the vision to make our church a house

of prayer, He warned me that if we attempted this, we needed to be willing to lose half our leadership team and half our congregation as a consequence. I thought it was just an Abraham/Isaac thing, that God just wanted to see our conviction. It turned out to be an actual prediction.

Once we started praying, within a short time, half my leadership team quit. Not because they thought praying was wrong; rather, they all believed that it was the right thing and hard thing to do, but it was costly. All the team members who moved on did so because they recognized the commitment needed and were honest that they weren't ready to do so. They didn't want to hold the church back, so they left. It was honest, but disheartening. It was not until I had prayed through it that I realized it was a blessing to have people who could not commit to prayer move on. What was left was a more desperate and dependent group.

These days we pray for everything in a bold expectant way. And God has answered so many prayers. At the same time, the spiritual warfare continues to ramp up. But we are not discouraged or deterred. In fact, I think we are slowly developing an audaciousness to our faith in prayer. It's been a long journey but a fruitful one.

So, we are still praying. We don't know what else to do anymore. That's a good thing!

God loves it when we spend time with Him in meaningful prayer. Our relationship with Him grows. He works in our lives. We also know that God has chosen prayer as a primary way of unleashing His power in people's lives. When God's people pray, amazing things happen. People come to Christ. They grow in their faith. They have the resources to live out God's call on their lives. God is glorified.

**What the Church needs today is not new organizations or more and novel methods,
but people whom the Holy Spirit can use - people of prayer, people mighty in prayer.**

(E.M. Bounds – paraphrased)

Reflection/Discussion Questions

1. What do you make of your church's "Prayer" score on the Church Discipleship Assessment (see login information at the end of the book)?

2. Watch the video *The Role of Prayer in Spiritual Awakening* by Dr. J. Edwin Orr (you can find it on YouTube at http://bit.ly/2yqX5tO). Apart from Dr. Orr's red suit and the poor video quality, what stands out to you from the video?

3. What do you notice about these revival accounts?

4. What can we apply from these stories to our ministries today?

5. What were some of your thoughts as you read about Pastor Chris' bold step to help his church become a praying church?

6. To see revival come, Jonathan Edwards said that we must have "explicit agreement and visible union of all God's people in extraordinary prayer." Imagine that five years have passed and your church has become a people of extraordinary prayer. Describe what you see in this praying church.

7. What specific steps would you need to take to help your church realize more of God's vision for a praying church?

8. What are some additional thoughts you have about strengthening prayer in your church?

Chapter 2

Growing Relationships

Growing relationships are an essential component of discipleship in the church. Without relational depth, discipleship suffers. Loving community is one in which people invest deeply in each other's lives.

In this chapter, we will look at eight characteristics of relationships in effective disciple-making communities.

Transparency

In a transparent community, people are open and real with one another. They share successes and struggles. They're not afraid to deal with tough questions. In fact, when this kind of transparency exists in a church, young people are much more likely to stick with the church as they move into adulthood (this is one of the key findings in the *Hemorrhaging Faith Study: Why & When Canadian Young Adults are Leaving, Staying & Returning to the Church*).

Investment

Developing deep relationships requires a significant

investment of time and energy. Are we willing to carve out this space in our busy lives? Of course, maintaining meaningful relationships takes time and effort. When we get close to people, we enter their world – a complex and sometimes messy place. Living in those spaces requires commitment!

For several years, my family and I participated in missional communities that met in homes. Some people called them "simple church." Yet, we discovered that even though the structure was simple, the life-on-life disciple-ship that took place was often complicated. Nonetheless, Jesus-followers in effective disciple-making communities are willing to embrace the messiness of other people's lives and invest deeply in them.

Levity

When we laugh and enjoy one another, we are in a much better position to go deeper with one another. Levity is the gateway to and moderator of the intensity that is often required for deep discipleship.

Intensity

We want to have fun together, but we also need a certain amount of intensity that will position us to press more deeply into one another's lives. For example, if someone is struggling with a temptation, we want to provide the necessary support and accountability to overcome that temptation.

Prayerfulness

Within effective disciple-making communities,

people pray for one another (the focus of the previous chapter). God works powerfully in people's lives as we pray to that end. In Ephesians 6:18, Paul describes how our prayers for others are an important part of their spiritual protection. E.M. Bounds has written:

**Prayer fills man's emptiness with God's fullness.
Prayer puts away man's poverty with God's riches.
Prayer puts away man's weakness with the coming of God's strength.
It banishes man's littleness with God's greatness.**

Intentionality

I sometimes take a haphazard approach to making disciples. I socialize and support, but do I intentionally try to turn conversations into disciple-making opportunities? Not always. We need be intentional in our everyday conversations. We can also set up structured mentoring sessions where we can help people take next steps more quickly. I will share how we can turn any conversation into a disciple-making opportunity in chapter ten.

Interdependence

I love the way some cultures value a healthy interdependence. I can be a lone ranger who likes to do things on my own. Yet, when I open myself up and rely on others, it's amazing how this can deepen relationships.

We will not grow as disciple-making communities until we recognize that we need one another. Throughout Scripture, we are commanded to practice "one anothers" like encourage one another, love one another, and admonish one another (doing a study on the full list of 59 "one anothers" in Scripture can help people recognize the importance of interdependence). To do these well, we need to be in healthy, interdependent relationships.

Missional Focus

We sometimes think that relationships will suffer if we have a missional focus that pushes us outward. Alan Hirsch, in *The Forgotten Ways: Reactivating the Missional Church*, disagrees. He uses the word "communitas" to describe missional communities that have

> **overcome their instincts to "huddle and cuddle" and to instead form themselves around a common mission that calls them onto a dangerous journey to unknown places – a mission that calls the church to shake off its collective securities and to plunge into the world of action, where its members will experience disorientation and marginalization but also where they encounter God and one another in a new way.**

When a group has an outward focus, it actually has the potential to grow closer to one another.

Obviously, there are other characteristics of growing relationships. Yet, the eight I have mentioned in this chapter provide a start as we think about how we might encourage our people to grow deeper with one another, so that we can make disciples within and outside those relationships in a maximum way.

Reflection/Discussion Questions

1. What do you make of your church's "Community" score on the Church Discipleship Assessment (see login information at the end of the book)?

2. Why are close relationships important for discipleship?

3. How have you personally experienced spiritual growth through close relationships with other Christians?

4. What other characteristics of relationships in effective disciple-making communities would you add to the list below?

   a. _____ Transparency
   b. _____ Investment
   c. _____ Levity
   d. _____ Intensity
   e. _____ Prayerfulness
   f. _____ Intentionality
   g. _____ Interdependence
   h. _____ Missional Focus
   i. _____ Other -
   j. _____ Other -
   k. _____ Other -

5. Thinking about your church or a smaller group within the church, how would you assess each of the characteristics in question #4 on a scale of 1-10 (with 1 being very weak and 10 being very strong)?

6. Pick one characteristic from the list above that you think would be the most strategic to grow in the next six months. How are you and the Holy Spirit going to work together to grow that area?

7. What are some additional thoughts you have about the nature of relationships in effective disciple-making communities?

Chapter 3

Growth Orientation

How do we cultivate a church culture where people actually want to grow in their affection for Christ and in their capacity to serve Him more effectively? Without a growth mindset, people will likely be satisfied with a mediocre distortion of biblical Christianity – "a standard churchy spirituality that doesn't require any real action, courage, or sacrifice" (Michael Frost and Allan Hirsch in *The Faith of Leap*).

A deep, disciple-making movement is possible when people grow in their relationship with God, develop godly character, pursue their God-given calling, love others, and hone and use their gifts/abilities in tandem with others.

In this chapter, I will share six ways that leaders can foster a growth mindset in their churches.

Share What You're Learning

Growing leaders inspire others to grow. We need to share humbly what we're learning from Scripture, what is helping us from our other reading and watching, and the lessons God is trying to teach us through our mistakes and successes. Be open and transparent about your journey.

Facilitate Learning Experiences

If you're a ministry leader, you must facilitate learning experiences for your ministry team. Regularly debrief with team members one-on-one and as a team to catch key lessons that will strengthen people and their ministry. Do training activities with your team, whether it's 15 minutes at the start of a meeting, a half-day of training on a Saturday morning or an annual retreat. Training ministries like MinistryLift (www.MinistryLift.ca) can help you provide training if you need assistance.

Provide Appropriate Resources that Build Capacity

As a ministry leader, be on the lookout for excellent resources that will build up your team. If you're a church board chair, you may want to purchase books for your board members and then spend time each board meeting working through some of the content. It's easy to pass along links to great blog articles, TED Talks and other easily accessible resources. I also like to look for person-specific resources that match the expressed needs of individual team members. Of course, we need to pass on only the best resources and to do so at an acceptable pace. We don't want to overwhelm people with too much good information!

Ask Good Coaching Questions

We can stimulate learning and growth through any conversation. Asking good questions can help people think in new and deeper ways. Here are four questions leaders can ask to expand people's thinking:

1. What are you learning from this experience?
2. How do you see God at work in this situation?
3. What are some options that you have not seriously considered yet?
4. What would you like this _____ (relation-ship, ministry, program, etc.) to look like in three years?

Develop a Personal Growth Plan

Personal growth plans are an excellent way of identifying key growth areas, charting out the necessary steps to achieve growth, and providing accountability to take those next steps. Here are three important steps to developing a plan that will help you and others in your church put feet to good intentions:

Step 1 - Identify one to three areas of your life where you would like to see change

Where would you like to grow? It's important that you identify specific growth targets. For example, you may want to grow spiritually over the next six months. That's great! Yet, I encourage you to think about a particular area of your spiritual life in which you would like to grow. For me, I would like to strengthen my prayer life. At this stage, we are expressing good intentions. In my experience, most people stop here. The next step is critical to translating the good intentions into life change.

Step 2 - Develop three to five SMART action steps around each area where you would like to see change

As you think about actions steps that you can take to develop the area(s) you identified in Step 1, make sure that they are SMART:

Specific (focused on one clearly defined area) – Regarding my desire to strengthen my prayer life, I would like one of my action steps to focus specifically on personal prayer retreats.

Measurable (you should be able to chart your progress and know when you have achieved the action step) – My first action step involves going on two one-day prayer retreats over the next six months.

Achievable (you should be able to achieve the action step by the end of the six months) – Action steps are kind of like baby steps. As you take them, you experience a sense of accomplishment, which creates the momentum necessary to take further steps. Regarding my prayer action step, my initial thought was to do monthly prayer retreats. However, I think once every three months is more doable.

Realistic (you should actually be able to do it given your commitments and other considerations) – We can dream up all sorts of wonderful goals and resolutions. Most of them fall by the wayside simply because they are not realistic given who we are and our other commitments. My prayer retreat goal is realistic given my other commitments.

Time-bound (you should include a completion date so that you have a clear target for completing the action step) – I encourage you to put this target completion date in your calendar and insert reminders in the preceding weeks to make sure it's on your radar.

My SMART action step is to set up (in the next week) two one-day prayer retreats that will take place over the next six months (one retreat every three months).

Step 3 - Set up supportive accountability

Share the area(s) of your life you would like to change and the accompanying action steps with someone who will pray for you and encourage you. Growth can be hard work and we need this kind of support to take the necessary steps.

Pray for God's Spirit to Work in People's Lives

Another key way to promote a growth mindset in your church is to pray for the Holy Spirit to work in people's lives. This is so critical. Hudson Taylor said it well: "We need to learn to move [people] through God by prayer alone." God responds to the prayers of His people and often does immeasurably more than we could ever ask or imagine. Now, this does not diminish the importance of the previous five ways of fostering a growth mindset (share what you're learning, facilitate learning experiences, pro-vide appropriate resources that build capacity, ask good coaching questions, and develop a personal growth plan), but it does put them in their proper place. Deep growth happens as God's Spirit moves in people's lives.

Abraham Maslow once said, "In any given moment we have two options: To step forward into growth or to step back into safety." As we and our people choose to step forward again and again, we will position the church for maximum growth and discipleship.

Reflection/Discussion Questions

1. What do you make of your church's "Growth Orientation" score on the Church Discipleship Assessment (see login information at the end of the book)?

2. Why is a growth orientation important for developing a church culture in which discipleship can flourish?

3. What are you learning these days?

4. What kinds of learning experiences have you found particularly effective for helping people grow?

5. What are some of the resources that you have passed along to others recently?

6. Thinking about a recent ministry event, come up with three debriefing questions that you could ask your ministry leaders that would help turn the ministry event into even more of a learning experience for them (and you)?

7. What is one area of your life where you would like to see growth? What would be a SMART action step that you could take in this area?

8. How could you use the personal growth plan to encourage growth in those involved in your ministry?

9. What other thoughts do you have about fostering a growth mindset in your church?

Chapter 4
Personalized Approach

My friend, Kajle Radbourne, once gave me a powerful metaphor for discipleship. Imagine a staircase that represents spiritual growth and maturity. One way to disciple would be for someone further up the staircase to call people on the lower steps to a higher standard and the application of that standard. This might be motivational. A similar approach would be for someone who is more spiritually mature to not only call others to a higher standard, but to provide a detailed plan about how to achieve that growth. That might be instructional.

What do you notice about these two approaches? They are both truth-based and growth-oriented. They provide an important vision for spiritual maturity. They communicate necessary ideas. Yet, they lack a personal touch and may not actually help a person take the next step in their discipleship journey.

A third approach would be for the disciple-maker to come alongside the disciple – to climb down the stairs and join them in their spiritual journey. This kind of personalized approach allows the disciple-maker to enter the experience of the disciple (and vice versa) and to provide the necessary support and guidance to take next steps.

What are some of the characteristics of this kind of personalized approach?

It Assumes Relationship

We cannot truly understand where people are at apart from a growing relationship with them. As we connect deeply with people, we can pray, encourage, support, and speak into their lives in ways that can help them move forward. We can develop the kinds of relationships that pave the way for effective discipleship as we saw in chapter two.

It Involves Customization

A large-group or programmatic approach to discipleship is often good for covering broad discipleship themes. A highly relational approach allows the disciplemaker to customize the application of this kind of content, so that it has maximum value for the other person.

It Necessitates a Coaching/Mentoring Mindset

A personalized approach to discipleship involves intentionally turning our conversations into mentoring opportunities. How can we partner with the Holy Spirit in what He wants to do in the other person's life? What questions can we ask that will nudge the other person toward a deeper awareness of their situation and the next steps they need to take (more on this in chapter ten)?

It Is Possible and Highly Desirable Within Structured Programs

One of my mentors once said, "So often, we only achieve balance as we swing, like a pendulum, from one extreme to the other." In the past, we have tried a programmatic approach to discipleship with mixed results. Yet, when programs provide a space where people can come alongside one another in the discipleship journey, they have a much greater potential for facilitating life change. We don't have to throw out programs, but can use them for communicating truth and building relational bridges that allow for in-depth discipleship.

Increasingly, Millennials and others crave a personalized approach to discipleship that helps them make sense of their current reality and take steps forward as followers of Jesus. Any disciple-making strategy must include this personal touch for maximum discipleship to occur.

Reflection/Discussion Questions

1. What do you make of your church's "Personalized Approach" score on the Church Discipleship Assessment (see login information at the end of the book)?

2. What has helped you mature as a Christian over the years?

3. As you look back over your spiritual journey, what might have helped you grow more?

4. As you think about the stair metaphor for discipling others, what would you say is your preferred approach for discipling others at this point?

5. What discipleship approach do you think would be most effective with the people you're trying to disciple?

6. What are the advantages of group-based discipleship (e.g. small group Bible studies, topical classes, worship services)? What are the disadvantages?

7. What are the disadvantages of a personalized approach to discipleship? What are the advantages?

8. What other thoughts do you have about adopting a personalized approach to discipleship?

Chapter 5

Missional Mindset

The early church, with all its missteps and doctrinal struggles, was an inspiring example of a missional church – a loving, Christ-centered church on a mission to be and make growing disciples of Jesus. What can we learn from the early church in Acts about being missional today?

Marks of a Missional Church

In Acts 2:42-47, we find a description of the early church – a church that was seeing people come to Christ regularly. What was going on?

The Early Christians were Devoted

The early church devoted themselves to the apostles' teaching, the fellowship, the breaking of bread, and prayer (Acts 2:42).

The Greek word for "devotion" means to give something our steadfast attention, to care for it relentlessly, and to wait courageously on something constantly. What were the objects of the early church's devotion?

They were devoted to learning truth according to

what the apostles taught. They learned and lived out the truth wholeheartedly and courageously.

They were devoted to the fellowship. They were committed to each other in an enduring sort of way.

They were committed to remembering Jesus. They broke bread regularly as a way of rallying to Christ, keeping him at the forefront of their lives.

They engaged in extraordinary prayer.

They were Filled with Awe

In the early church, "Everyone was filled with awe, and many wonders and miraculous signs were done by the apostles" (Acts 2:43).

The people were amazed at what God was doing in, through and around them. It was a powerful time when God regularly demonstrated His power. When God is working in us and through us, there is always evidence to show that He is at work. Sometimes, we miss it. Yet, as we take the time to notice and give thanks to the Lord, we will be amazed at the miracles that God is performing in and around us.

They Did Life Together

All the believers were together and had everything in common (Acts 2:44). We get the impression that the early Christians enjoyed a strong sense of community. They were close to each other. They helped each other. They met together in large and small groups. They were together in their relationships and in their sense of mission for Jesus.

They were Happy

The believers were happy. Wouldn't we be happy, too, if we were experiencing this kind of vibrant, intimate, Christ-centered, truth-inspired, prayer-driven, and awe-inspiring community?

God Gave the Christians Favor with Others

God was powerfully at work in the church in Acts. Part of this work was granting the Christians favor in the eyes of those around them (Acts 2:47). This favor was an important part of people receiving the gospel message and accepting Jesus.

People Came to Christ

The passage in Acts continues: "And the Lord added to their number daily those who were being saved" (Acts 2:47).

Why did people become Christians so readily in the early church? Obviously, God was working in a powerful way. People were committed to the truth – the truth being Jesus Himself and His teachings. When we live out the truth, when we live out Jesus and His teachings, it's a powerful testimony to those around us.

In addition, intimate community sends a strong and attractive message of love to those who see it. Jesus said in John 13:35, "By this everyone will know that you are my disciples, if you love one another."

I suspect that the loving, Christ-centered, joyful, and prayerful community of the early church was instrumental in pointing people to Jesus.

Applying What We See in the Early Church Today

Now, fast forward to today. How do we take what we see in the early church and apply it as we attempt to reach people today with the gospel?

A Missional Church is Incarnational

A missional church recognizes that most people will not come to a building to hear the gospel. People in a missional church are actively bringing Christ to those who desperately need him. Just as "the Word became flesh and blood and moved into the neighborhood" (John 1:14 – The Message), we, too, are compelled to live in an incarnational way and lovingly share the gospel with those around us.

For the past 18 years, we have lived in a nine-unit townhouse complex. Even though we've contemplated buying a detached house many times, one of the main reasons that we stay in the complex is because it's easier to do life with people when you live close to them. It's definitely harder to avoid your neighbor when they're standing 10 feet away (although we do manage to do this sometimes). Over the years, we've shared the gospel with several of our townhouse friends. At least two of them have accepted Christ.

We took this living in close proximity idea one step further a while back when we moved into an apartment building with refugees for seven months. We did life with these newcomers to Canada and had many opportunities to share Christ. In fact, it was sometimes ridiculously easy to talk about our faith.

I remember an experience we had with one of the Muslim refugee couples. We were visiting one night and the husband was sharing how he had been attending a local church to learn English and make contacts. He quite liked the services, but was confused about one thing. What were those little cups of juice and crackers all about?

That night, my wife and I had the privilege of sharing the meaning behind those communion elements – how Jesus died for our sins and rose again from the dead.

Of course, not everyone lives in an apartment or a townhouse. The point is that we need to find ways to move into people's lives – to build relationships, to be a blessing and to share the gospel as the Holy Spirit opens people's hearts to hear it.

Here are six ways that anyone can share their faith:

Pray

Several years ago, a guest speaker at our church preached on the importance of praying for the unsaved people in our lives. He challenged us to pray for five unsaved neighbors, five minutes a day, five days a week, and to do it for five weeks. He encouraged us to BLESS our unsaved friends and family by praying for their:

Bodies – Health, protection, strength
Labor – Work, income, security
Emotions – Joy, peace, comfort
Social life – Marriage, family, friends
Spiritual life – Salvation

As the five weeks of praying regularly for my unsaved neighbors turned into months and years, I was amazed at how God answered those prayers. The two neighbors I mentioned previously were on my prayer list.

As Hudson Taylor once said, "We need to learn to move [people] through God by prayer alone."

Love Each Other

When Christians love each other (I'm talking about a deep, sacrificial, life-on-life kind of love), it sends a powerful signal to a world desperate for love.

Be a Blessing

I remember walking to church one Sunday morning. I was a pastor at the time. One of my neighbors came out of his house just as I was walking by. He was in his painting clothes and seemed quite agitated. He shared with me that he was hard-pressed to get some painting done before a contractor arrived to do some work for him later that day. Part of me wanted to help, but I couldn't just abandon my church responsibilities. I wished him well and continued my trek to church.

Even though I probably couldn't have helped my neighbor right then and there, I realized that I had become rather selfish in my interactions with my neighbors. I didn't really want to get involved in their lives. That day marked a turning point as I attempted to be more of a blessing to my neighbors.

Being a blessing to others can be as simple as giving them a smile, taking the time to talk, wheeling an empty garbage can back to someone's garage, being extra polite to the restaurant server and so on.

I remember a news story a few years ago about a Winnipeg public bus driver who saw a homeless man on the side of the road. He stopped the bus, took off his shoes, and gave them to the man. This act of kindness went viral and made the national news. Our society is not used to blessing others in these kinds of ways so when it happens, people notice.

Build Relationships

Of course, one of the best ways to bless others is to befriend them. Jesus said to love our neighbors even as we love ourselves (Mark 12:30-31). As we build relationships with unsaved people, they will see Jesus up close in our lives.

Tell Your Faith Story

All Christians have a story about the difference Jesus has made and is making in their lives. Don't be afraid to share it as a natural expression of something that's very important to you. If someone gave me a million dollars, I daresay I would want to share the news with people. God has given us something far more valuable – a fulfilling life both now and forever.

Share the Gospel

I remember when we shared the gospel with Cathie, a dear friend and someone who had been on our prayer list for a long time. When we asked her whether she wanted to pray to receive Christ, she didn't have to think long before saying, "Yes!" God had prepared her heart. She was ready.

The salvation message is very simple. God loves everyone. Yet, because of our sin, there is a break in the relationship between God and us. Jesus, God's Son, died for our sin and rose from the dead. He took the punishment we deserve. Those who accept Jesus as their Savior from sin and who make him Lord of their lives become children of God forever.

You and I can share this message in conversation with others. There are also tools that can help. Power to Change and the Billy Graham Evangelistic Association have book-lets that we can use to share the message. I have used an approach called "Napkin Evangelism" for years where I share the gospel on a napkin or a piece of paper. I also have an app called "God Tools" on my phone that goes through Four Spiritual Truths.

I truly believe that all of us can share Christ with others by praying, loving each other, blessing people, building relationships, telling our faith stories and sharing the gospel.

A missional church is incarnational, but how do we free people up from focusing too much on personal pursuits, Christian relationships, and even church activities so that they can more fully embrace the unsaved around them?

A Missional Church Equips and Empowers Individuals to be Active in their Harvest Fields

It's one thing to talk about being a missional church, but how do we mobilize the masses to live missionally?

Let me suggest five ways:

1. Sermons need to remind people of the importance of the gospel for both them and the unsaved. This gives people a vision for gospel living.

2. People need to hear salvation testimonies and stories about people who are actively reaching out to the lost. This gives people a passion for gospel living.

3. Small groups need to make outreach one of their primary purposes (more on this in chapter nine). This gives people the necessary support and accountability for gospel living.

4. Training in evangelism and apologetics gives people the tools they might need to share the gospel. Of course, anyone who has accepted Christ should be able to help someone do the same thing. Yet, training helps to empower people and can touch on topics (e.g. objections to Christianity) that can help in witnessing.

5. Outreach oriented programs can provide a bridge into the community (e.g. Alpha, TESOL, children and youth programs). That same bridge can help unsaved people or new Christians move closer to the heart of the church community. Even as we develop a strong outreach focus in our church programs, we need to remember that they will only attract a small percentage of the unchurched population. Unsaved people need meaningful relationships with individuals in your church who can live and share the gospel with them in loving and respectful ways.

Let me conclude with some words from Allan Hirsch in his book, *The Forgotten Ways: Reactivating the Missional Church*:

If we're going to impact our world in the name of Jesus, it will be because people like you and me took action in the power of the Spirit. Ever since the mission and ministry of Jesus, God has never stopped calling for a movement of 'Little Jesuses' to follow him into the world and unleash the remarkable redemptive genius that lies in the very message we carry. Given the situation of the Church in the West, much will now depend on whether we are willing to break out of a stifling herd instinct and find God again in the context of the advancing kingdom of God.

In these first five chapters, we've looked at several church cultural elements that can provide a context in which disciple-making flourishes. If we do not intentionally grow these areas, it is unlikely that the other disciple-making elements we discuss will have significant impact.

In the next two chapters, we will examine two types of large group disciple making: biblical and engaging preaching and effective group training.

Reflection/Discussion Questions

1. What do you make of your church's "Missional Mind-set" score on the Church Discipleship Assessment (see login information at the end of the book)?

2. Which Scriptures have motivated you to reach out to unsaved people?

3. Why do you think the early church regularly saw people coming to Christ?

4. Why do you think most churches in North America do not see many people coming to Christ?

5. What's different about the churches in North America or other parts of the world that are seeing people accept Christ all the time?

6. Who are five unsaved people in your life that you want to see come to Christ?

   a.

   b.

   c.

   d.

   e.

7. Would you be willing to pray for them for five minutes a day, five days a week, for five weeks (and see how God responds to those prayers)?

8. As you think about the five ways for mobilizing people to live missionally (gospel preaching, salvation testimonies and stories about reaching out to unsaved people, small groups making outreach a key priority, training in evangelism and apologetics, and outreach oriented programs), which ones are stronger in your church? Which ones are weaker?

9. Pick one of the five ways for mobilizing people to live missionally (or another one that you identify) that you would like to strengthen as a way of strategically moving the church forward in mission. What practical steps could you take in the next six months to build this area?

10. What other thoughts do you have about developing a missional mindset in your church?

Chapter 6
Biblical and Engaging Preaching

Even though we want to make disciples in such a way that we help everyone take next steps, in this chapter, I'm going to focus on preaching to Millennials. They represent a significant part of the present and future church. As you will see, many of the principles and ideas in this chapter also apply to other generations.

When we first moved to Thailand, I would sometimes get frustrated when trying to purchase items in local shops. I didn't know Thai and the shopkeepers usually didn't know English. Invariably, I would speak louder and slower to make them understand me. Most of the time, they didn't and I would become more and more frustrated. Looking back, the problem was pretty obvious – we spoke different languages!

Millennials represent an age grouping born between 1980-2000 (give or take a few years, depending on who you read). Their preferred language of communication is often different from what the rest of the population uses. Yet, those of us not in the Millennial age grouping often continue to preach in a "language" that Millennials struggle to fully understand or relate to. Just like in my Thailand example, both sides get frustrated because of the language difference.

Millennials hold many values, but seven core values that are common to many of them are diversity, collaboration, authenticity, entrepreneurship, holistic integration, community, and open-source (see Geoff Kullman's description of these values in his book, *Engage Millennials*).

In light of these seven core values, how can we effectively preach to Millennials? Let me offer ten suggestions related to sermon preparation and delivery.

Walk Closely with Jesus

Whether it's Millennials or anyone else, people notice and respond to preachers who are connected to Christ. It's one thing when we speak about something with which we are vaguely familiar; it's quite another when we speak about something that flows out of a renovated life. Millennials are particularly good at spotting the real goods.

Collaborate with Millennials and Others to Discern Sermon Topics and Content

Millennials love to participate in setting direction for virtually anything. Capitalize on this desire by enlisting their help to discern sermon topics and content. Even if you or the church leadership team chooses a series focus (e.g. "Discerning Your God-given Calling"), seek the input of Millennials as to the questions/concerns they have related to the main topic. Millennials are more likely to engage with a sermon when they have contributed to it in some way.

Acknowledge and Explore Diverse Perspectives

We all have our biases. Consequently, our sermons (and any other form of communication) will always have a certain tilt. Millennials appreciate it when we go outside our usual way of looking at things and include different perspectives. In addition, be open about theological tensions. For example, I once heard a sermon on hell that clearly outlined a biblical position on the physical reality of eternal punishment, but also addressed arguments against this interpretation of Scripture. This approach draws Millennials into the discovery process because it includes diverse perspectives. As a result, the sermon becomes more believable.

Tackle Tough Questions

One of the reasons that young adults leave the church is because church leaders avoid addressing tough questions (see the *Hemorrhaging Faith Study: Why & When Canadian Young Adults are Leaving, Staying & Returning to the Church*). A few years ago, our church did a series on *Hard Questions* that addressed topics like the *Creation/Evolution Debate* and *A Christian View and Response to Homosexuality*. It was a terrific way of exploring a biblical perspective on several hot topics.

Go Deep in Scripture

Contrary to what some might think, Millennials want to get into the heart of Scripture. Don't be afraid to go deep with a passage or topic. Millennials tend to be broad-minded and appreciate hearing how various Scriptures add to one's understanding about a topic (and how other biblical themes might intersect with the topic at hand).

Weave Story and Metaphor into Your Content

What do we do when we get together with friends? We often swap stories. This is a primary way of communicating in many cultures. Preachers would do well to weave engaging stories throughout their sermons as a way of tapping into this well-accepted way of communicating.

Incorporate Relevant and Appropriate Media

Where do we often go when we're not sure how to fix something? I don't know about you, but YouTube is often my first stop. In most cases, I've found that someone has made a video that shows me exactly how to solve my problem. We live in a media age and so it makes sense to include meaningful media elements in our sermons.

I should add that we are currently experiencing a counter-trend where some people have become over-saturated with media. They are craving minimalist sermons that use media sparingly. We should monitor the strength of this sentiment within our current and target audiences, and adjust our approach accordingly.

Share Personal Struggles

Be real in the pulpit. Share deeply how you have struggled with and applied the truths you are sharing. When we come across as having everything together, some people may get discouraged because they know they cannot live up to their perception of our perfection. It's much easier to follow the example of someone who struggles just like us.

Facilitate Reflection and Interaction Around Key Ideas

It's important that we give people a chance to think and apply what the Holy Spirit might be saying to them. This could be as simple as giving people a one-minute opportunity at the end of the sermon to identify what God wants them to take away from the message.

In addition, Millennials love exploring truth in community. Facilitating interaction during the sermon (e.g. meeting around tables for discussion) or after a sermon (e.g. mid-week small group discussions about sermon content) can provide a context where the Holy Spirit can apply truth in a deeper way in people's lives.

Adopt a Relational Approach

Preachers who come across as lawyers or salespeople do not usually gain much of an audience with Millennials. Be friendly. Speak conversationally. Love people through your words and actions.

Even though I've focused on preaching to Millennials in this chapter, these suggestions are also applicable to ministering to older and younger generations (some to a lesser degree than others). Of course, preaching is not adequate in and of itself to make disciples. However, it is an important element in developing a strategic approach to discipleship in many churches where the worship service is a central gathering point.

Reflection/Discussion Questions

1. What do you make of your church's "Biblical and Engaging Preaching" score on the Church Discipleship Assessment (see login information at the end of the book)?

2. In your view, what role does preaching play in making disciples?

3. What are some examples of preaching styles that do not connect well with most Millennials?

4. What have you found as a preacher or seen in other preachers that is effective in connecting with Millennials?

5. Take a moment to assess how you and/or your preaching team is doing with the 10 characteristics of effective preaching to Millennials (with 1 being very weak and 10 being very strong).

   a. _____ Walk closely with Jesus
   b. _____ Collaborate with Millennials and others to discern sermon topics and content
   c. _____ Acknowledge and explore diverse perspectives
   d. _____ Tackle tough questions
   e. _____ Go deep in Scripture
   f. _____ Weave story and metaphor into your content
   g. _____ Incorporate relevant and appropriate

		media
h.	_____	Share personal struggles
i.	_____	Facilitate reflection and interaction around key themes
j.	_____	Adopt a relational approach

6. If you were to purposefully strengthen one of the ten characteristics (or a different one that you think is important), which one would it be?

7. What are three steps you could take in the next three months to strengthen this area?

8. How do you balance preaching to Millennials with preaching to the other age categories in your congregation?

9. What other thoughts do you have about biblical preaching as a way of making disciples?

Chapter 7

Effective Group Training

Effective training in the church is an important discipleship element. Our training should help people grow in their relationship with Jesus, develop godly character, understand and live out their calling, grow deeper in their relationships, serve more effectively on ministry teams, and/or help them increase their knowledge and sharpen their skills so they can better live out their calling.

What are the characteristics of training that equips people in these key discipleship areas?

Effective Training Starts with the Trainer

The effectiveness of the training is largely dependent on four aspects related to the trainers themselves:

1. Their hearts - Are they growing in their relationship with Jesus and increasingly demonstrating Christ-like qualities?
2. Their knowledge - Are they offering well-researched and well-thought out ideas?
3. Their skill - Are they good learning facilitators?
4. Their preparedness - Are they physically and

emotionally healthy? Have they prayed over the content and the learners? Are they discerning about what the learners need?

When trainers attend well to these four areas, they position themselves to train in transformational ways.

Effective Training is Relational

Trainers who want to equip others care about people. They train in a relational way that demonstrates learner sensitivity. This involves choice of words, body language (e.g. tone of voice, proximity to learners, gestures) and even room set-up. Mentoring occurs both in and outside of the learning venues. Learners feel like they're being "pastored" by relational trainers as they interact with them.

Effective Training is Engaging

Trainers who want to have a significant impact engage their listeners through creative teaching methods. They help make the content relevant (and help the learners see its relevance). They drive towards knowledge application. This is often done through active learning where learners interact with others about key ideas. Building in group discussions and other group activities helps draw people into the learning process.

Effective Training is Transformational

Disciple-making trainers stimulate critical, constructive thinking that paves the way for transformation. They ask good questions that expand people's thinking. They present ideas that take people in new directions. Ultimately, they make way for the Holy Spirit to do the deeper work of heart transformation.

Effective Training Helps People Reflect and Process in Deeper Ways

We often don't give people enough time to adequately process information. I remember attending a conference one time where I decided that I wouldn't attend additional sessions until I had carefully processed what I had already heard. This meant arriving late for some sessions and even skipping others. Yet, by the end of the conference, I found that I had captured some important ideas that I might have missed if I had hurried from one session to the next.

It's important that we build in opportunities for personal reflection. This can happen in small group discussions or we can give people time at the end of a session to record their insights and what they're going to do with them.

In this chapter and the previous one, we've seen that preaching and training are two important group approaches to making disciples. In the next chapter, we'll look at how small groups can provide an excellent forum for disciple-making.

Reflection/Discussion Questions

1. What do you make of your church's "Effective Group Training" score on the Church Discipleship Assessment (see login information at the end of the book)?

2. What kind of group training do you already do in your church (e.g. ministry leader training, leadership retreats, adult education classes)?

3. Thinking about what you already do with group training, how do you see it helping with discipleship in your church?

4. Which of the five characteristics of effective group training (starts with the trainer, relational, engaging, transformational, helps people reflect and process in deeper ways) are already strengths with the group training you offer? Which ones are weaker?

5. How might you further strengthen group training as a way of equipping people to love God more deeply and serve Him more effectively in your church?

6. How might you use group training to bridge with the unsaved in your community thus leveraging group training for missional impact?

7. Thinking about the six discipleship growth areas listed below, which areas could benefit from more group training in your church? What kinds of training might you offer to strengthen those areas?

   a. Grow in their relationship with Jesus
   b. Develop godly character
   c. Understand and live out their calling
   d. Grow deeper in their relationships
   e. Serve more effectively on ministry teams
   f. Increase knowledge and sharpen skills so they can better live out their calling

8. What other thoughts do you have about practical training as a way of making disciples?

Chapter 8

Robust Small Groups

Most churches have small groups that meet for prayer, Bible study, and fellowship. Yet, many of those groups have reached a plateau. Group members are vulnerable with one another to a certain point. They hold each other accountable to a certain point. They engage in ministry to one another and to others outside their group to a certain point.

This is not to say that good things are not happening in these groups. Yet, many Christians long for more. They crave deep community, life-on-life discipleship, and missional impact that makes a significant difference in the world around them.

A 2011 study on small groups entitled, *Small Groups - Big Impact: Connecting People to God and One Another in Thriving Groups* by Jim Egli and Dwight Marable, provides helpful guidance for taking our groups to the next level. Egli and Marable discovered that groups that see people accept Christ, increase in size, and multiply into additional groups have four things in common: they have small group leaders who model and facilitate prayer, outreach, care and the empowerment of group members.

Prayer

Egli and Marable's study found that 83% of groups that had a leader who modelled and facilitated prayer saw someone come to Christ in the past nine months (compared to 19% of groups that did not have a praying leader).

Praying leaders spend time with God. They actively pray for group members and group meetings. They pray for unsaved people in their lives and in the lives of others within the group.

As the leader and others in the group engage in a lifestyle of prayer, people sense God's presence in the group. Life change happens. People get saved. Wouldn't you want to be part of that kind of group?

Outreach

When group leaders and their groups have an outreach focus, they are much more likely to see people come to Christ. The study found that 90% of groups with this kind of intentional focus saw someone come to Christ in the last six months (compared to 11% of groups without this outreach emphasis). In their book, Egli and Marable talked about the five I's of reaching out:

1. **Investment** - Members spend time with friends in order to share Christ
2. **Invitation** – Leaders encourage members to invite others to the regular meeting or group social events
3. **Intention** - Outreach is a stated purpose of the group
4. **Intercession** – Group members pray during

their meetings for unsaved friends

5. **Imitation** - Leaders model relational outreach

Some churches are moving toward a missional community model within their small group ministry. Missional communities strive to mobilize their members into incarnational living – to take Jesus and the gospel into their neighborhoods, schools, workplaces and other natural networks. Often these groups will also focus on a disciple-making mission that God has entrusted to them as a group (e.g. reaching the refugees in their community). In the church we attend, we are currently in the process of starting a missional community. We're excited about how God will use these kinds of communities to make disciples in a maximum way.

Care

A strong caring orientation is another key strategy for growing our small groups. The study showed that 44% of caring groups added at least four new members since they started (compared to 18% without this emphasis). Caring groups spend time with one another outside of group meetings. They pray for each other, support each other, and have fun together. Group members function like a family.

People sometimes assume that they will sacrifice group intimacy if their small group focuses on outreach. Egli and Marable found that the opposite was true. "If you want to experience deeper community in your small group, you should make it an open group that actively reaches out to others" (p. 37).

Empowerment

Growing groups often have group leaders who empower group members to live out God's calling on their lives (62% of groups with empowering leaders had multiplied or sent out new leaders versus 27% of groups without an empowering leader). They see the potential in people and encourage members to take risks to realize their potential. They are constantly looking for and developing leaders who will be able to lead the existing group and possibly lead a new group in the future.

As we have been working on starting a missional community at our church, we have tried to carefully incorporate these four elements into the DNA of these groups. We have identified five core values that we want to grow in these communities (notice how they align with the four strategies for growing a small group that we've explored in this chapter):

1. **Outreach** – Missional communities strive to mobilize their members into incarnational living – to take Jesus and the gospel into our neighborhoods, schools, workplaces, and other natural networks.

2. **In-depth, Multigenerational Discipleship** – We want to help each other grow in Christ at an optimal pace. We believe that multigenerational communities can provide a great space for this to happen. We want to make growing disciples who make other growing disciples – to contribute to a disciple-making movement in our church and elsewhere.

3. **Loving Community** – We are called to practice the "one anothers" of Scripture 24/7. We want to be a continuous community that builds one another up, encourages one another, prays for one another, admonishes one another, and loves one another during and between our weekly gatherings. We also believe that community is enhanced when we rally together around our mission. The mission helps us to focus our energies in the most productive directions.

4. **Prayer Saturation** – We know that nothing of eternal value happens apart from God moving in people's lives. We desire to develop a strong prayer focus as a community and as individuals, so that we can encounter God in deeper ways and see Him move powerfully in and through us.

5. **Gift-oriented Ministry** – We want every member of our missional community, irrespective of age or gender, to use their gifts in a maximum way. We commit to supporting, equipping, and empowering people to live out their God-given calling.

Egli and Marable's research has been extremely helpful to me as I think about growing small groups. Yet, they offer a word of caution. In their research, they discovered that churches with thriving small group ministries had groups that practiced these four strategies (prayer, outreach, care, and empowerment), but they also had three elements within the larger church culture that supported these strategies:

1. **Intercession** – Churches with a strong small group ministry have a culture of prayer (sounds like chapter one all over again). The pastor models a life of prayer and communicates its importance through sermons and in other ways. Church leaders emphasize prayer and fasting. The congregation regularly experiences and hears stories of answered prayer including miraculous healings. It's easy to find opportunities to pray with others. God moves powerfully in this kind of praying church.

2. **Coaching** – Marable and Egli found that churches with thriving small group ministries emphasize coaching of small group leaders. A coach meets with small group leaders individually and as a group for support, prayer, and growth-oriented inter-actions. The coach is aware of small group leaders and prays regularly for them. As the small group leaders grow, so do their groups.

3. **Equipping** – Churches with healthy, growing small groups have a growth orientation (see chapter three). They're always looking for ways to equip people to love and serve God. They have a clear equipping system and are constantly developing new leaders.

Marable and Egli used the analogy of a tree to bring these three elements and the four strategies together. The three elements of intercession, coaching, and equipping are the roots of the tree. The four strategies (prayer, outreach, care, empower) are like the tree trunk and branches. The fruit of the tree is people coming to Christ, people welcomed into small groups, and groups multiplying to reach and disciple more people.

As we develop a culture of prayer, coaching, and equipping, our small groups will be better able to pray, care, empower, and reach out to the unsaved. The result – new and growing disciples of Jesus who are actively making new and growing disciples of Jesus in loving, Christ-centered community.

Reflection/Discussion Questions

1. What do you make of your church's "Robust Small Groups" score on the Church Discipleship Assessment (see login information at the end of the book)?

2. Thinking about your current small group (or a former one if you're not in a group right now), how do/did you encourage prayer in and for your group?

3. How might you strengthen outreach at the individual and group level?

4. How does your group care for each other? What is one way that your group could grow in this area?

5. What is your reaction to the quote below from Marable and Egli (p. 37)?

6. "If you want to experience deeper community in your small group, you should make it an open group that actively reaches out to others."

7. Here's a simple approach to empowering people in your group. List three people in your group and write down one idea beside each name as to how you could help them grow.

   a. Person #1 –

   b. Person #2 –

c. Person #3 –

8. Think about your small group's effectiveness in following the four strategies for growing a small group (prayer, outreach, care, empower). Using a scale of 1-10 (with 1 being very weak and 10 being very strong), assess each area.

   a. _____ - Prayer
   b. _____ - Outreach
   c. _____ - Care
   d. _____ - Empowering

9. You can do a free assessment of your small group on Jim Egli's website: http://jimegli.com/assessment/. MinistryLift also provides a small groups assessment:

   http://www.ministrylift.ca/small-groups-assessment

10. Pick one of the four strategies that you would like focus on in a special way. What are three steps you could take in the next month to strengthen that area in your small group? How would you strengthen that area in all the small groups in your church?

11. As you think about the three cultural elements for supporting a thriving small group ministry (inter-cession, coaching, equipping), which one is the strongest in your church? Which is the weakest? What three things could you do to strengthen these elements over the next year?

12. What other thoughts do you have about robust small groups as a way of making disciples?

Chapter 9
Supportive Accountability

"Genuine spirituality lives and flourishes only in cultures and relationships of accountability" (Reggie McNeal, in *Missional Renaissance*). If this is true, and I believe it is, then accountability must be an essential element of our disciple-making strategies.

I've included accountability as a small group element. However, accountability can also occur in large groups, one-on-one coaching relationships, and in our individual practice of spiritual disciplines.

Accountability, according to Dr. Dave Currie, is "the volunteer surrender of your life to the regular and frequent scrutiny and encouragement of another person for the purpose of ongoing life transformation that brings glory to God" (this quote is from an unpublished manuscript, *Getting SAPPY: The Power of a Spiritual Accountability Partner*).

Currie believes that this kind of accountability helps people gain perspective on current problems. It paves the way for support in tough times. It provides a consistent challenge to grow. It helps keep us focused on the future and on taking necessary next steps in our personal growth. In the words of Bob Proctor, "Accountability is the glue that ties commitment to the result."

Now, it's important to realize that the most effective forms of accountability combine loving graciousness with tenacious and consistent support. Accountability should not be legalistic or brutal. It's meant to provide just enough pressure to initiate and sustain growth at an optimal pace.

So, what does accountability look like? Often, it's simply discussing what's going on in our lives. What are our current struggles? What are the possibilities that excite us? It's talking about the emotions that we experience, particularly those that are recurring emotions. Account-ability provides an opportunity to explore our primary relationships. It's a place to ask hard questions.

Neil Cole, in his book *Cultivating a Life for God*, shares many accountability questions that people can ask each other in what he calls "Life Transformation Groups" (groups of two or three Christians that meet weekly to help each other grow in their relationship with God). Cole includes the following questions from James Bryan Smith and Richard Foster:

1. In what ways did God make His presence known to you since our last meeting? What experiences of prayer, meditation, and spiritual reading has God given you? What difficulties or frustrations did you encounter? What joys or delights?

2. What temptations did you face since our last meeting? How did you respond? Which spiritual disciplines did God use to lead you further into holiness of heart and life?

3. Have you sensed any influence or work of the Holy Spirit since our last meeting? What spiritual gifts did the Spirit enable you to exercise? What was the outcome? What fruit of the Spirit would you like to see increase in your life? What disciplines might be useful in this effort?

4. What opportunities did God give you to serve others since our last meeting? How did you respond? Did you encounter injustice to or oppression of others? Were you able to work for justice and shalom?

5. In what ways did you encounter Christ in your reading of the Scripture since our last meeting? How has the Bible shaped the way you think and live? Did God provide an opportunity for you to share your faith with someone? How did you respond?

Now, these are deep questions! We can ask much simpler ones like, "What is God telling you to do?" and "What are you going to do about it?" We can also adopt an action-oriented coaching approach that has accountability built into it (see the next chapter for more on this approach).

It is also possible to use the ancient practice, *Daily Examen*, individually or in a group as an accountability exercise. Prayerfully reflect on the following questions as you look back over your day or week:

1. Where do I recognize God's presence?

2. Where was God's Spirit touching me or someone else?

3. In my thoughts and actions, when was I the most Christ-like?

4. When did I fall short?

As you respond to these questions, be encouraged by your steps of obedience. Accept God's gracious forgiveness for sinful actions. Decide to be more aware of God's presence tomorrow and to live as He would have you live. Be thankful for what God has shown you.

I have found that the best places for accountability are in one-on-one relationships and small groups. One-on-one coaching that incorporates a call to action and subsequent accountability can be very helpful for taking necessary next steps.

For years, I have been in small groups that provided mutual support as we identified growth areas. Some groups were better at this than others. However, when people trust one another and have a desire to grow, you can build intentional accountability into a group to accelerate the growth process.

Stephen Covey said,

"Accountability breeds response-ability."

We need the loving support of others to take necessary actions. It's an essential ingredient in effective disciple-making.

Reflection/Discussion Questions

1. What do you make of your church's "Supportive Accountability" score on the Church Discipleship Assessment (see login information at the end of the book):

   www.ministrylift.ca/Church-Discipleship-Assessment.

2. What have been your positive and negative experiences with accountability?

3. What kinds of accountability are counterproductive and even harmful?

4. When does accountability work well in discipleship?

5. How could you strengthen the accountability dynamic in your small group? In your mentoring and coaching relationships?

6. What would a chapter on accountability be without asking some good accountability questions? Prayerfully respond to the *Daily Examen* questions below as you think about the last 24 hours. If you're doing these questions as a group, I encourage you to share your responses with one another.

   a. Where do I recognize God's presence?
   b. Where was God's Spirit touching me or someone else?
   c. In my thoughts and actions, when was I the most Christ-like?
   d. When did I fall short?

Note: As I mentioned in this chapter, take time to be thankful for the progress you see, accept God's forgiveness for missteps, and resolve to go deeper in your intimacy with God and further in your obedience to Him.

7. What other thoughts do you have about accountability as an important ingredient in the disciple-making process?

Chapter 10

Coaching/Mentoring

Wouldn't it be great if we could turn most of our conversations into disciple-making opportunities? In this chapter, we will look at four skills for turning any conversation into a disciple-making opportunity in a natural, conversational kind of way. In addition, we will explore a results-oriented approach to coaching that you can use in your structured coaching conversations.

Four Coaching Skills

The four skills we need to turn any conversation into a "covert" disciple-making opportunity are active listening, asking good questions, focusing on what is most important, and empowering people to take next steps.

Skill #1 – Active Listening

We all know that listening is important. Yet, most leaders are not listeners. We typically pre-conclude and make recommendations because we think it's more efficient. Leaders like to fix people and things quickly!

Active listening is holding off judgment and really trying to hear what the other person is actually saying and even thinking. To do this, we need to practice the 80/20 rule – listen 80% of the time and only talk 20%.

Five tips for listening better are:

1. **Listen with your mind** – Pay attention to what the other person is saying. Don't let your mind drift to other matters, even though they may be pressing.

2. **Listen with your body** – We all know that our body language often communicates more than our words. Active listening means that we are facing the person and maintaining appropriate eye contact (and not looking at our cell phone).

3. **Listen with your words** – It's important to sometimes summarize what you think the other person is saying, so that you know you're hearing correctly (and so the other person knows you are listening and care about the conversation).

4. **Listen with your intuition** – As you are listening, you will sometimes begin to "hear" things beneath the surface. Your intuition will notice subtle cues that will help you say things that nudge the conversation in productive directions.

5. **Listen with the Spirit** – As Christians, we have the Holy Spirit to guide us. Ask Him to give you insight into the conversation and then to guide you as to what to say.

I will sometimes do an activity with groups where I show them a picture of a man sitting on a wooden pew by himself in a church. His back is to us, but we can see that he is bundled up with a warm coat and a toque. I then ask the group: "What do you see?" "What's happening in this person's life?"

When I do this activity, I usually get a broad range of answers. Some people read loneliness or even desperation into the picture. Others see someone praying or warming up in a church building. Occasionally, someone will quip that the person obviously forgot about the time change!

Just like you, I don't know anything about this picture except what I see. Interestingly, even though we know little about the situation portrayed in the picture, we are quick to read into it based on our perceptions. These perceptions are sometimes accurate, but often they are misguided or at least incomplete. As we listen to others, it's important that we monitor our perceptions so that we do not come to conclusions prematurely.

Skill #2 – Asking Good Questions

Asking good questions can expand people's awareness and help them think in different ways. As Terry Walling, Executive Director of Leader Breakthru, said, "Discovery is about ownership. That which an individual discovers, they have a greater propensity to implement."

Good questions are open-ended. Instead of asking, "Did you feel angry when John left the group?" you could ask, "What was going on inside of you when John left the group?"

Questions that expand peoples' awareness are also pure questions that do not lead people in a certain direction. Instead of asking, "How do you think your negative attitude is hindering your leadership?" you might ask, "What are some things in your leadership approach that you feel may be holding your leadership back?"

Some of our casual conversations only last a minute or less. Can we really make disciples in such a short time? Imagine that you are talking to someone in the church lobby after a service. Here are some questions that you could ask to drive the conversation a bit deeper:

1. What's new in your life?
2. How's your family?
3. How are things at work (or school)?
4. What are you learning these days (or what has God been teaching you lately)?
5. How can I pray for you this week?

I also find that questions that follow-up on previous conversations or prior knowledge can take a conversation to a deeper level (e.g. "I was praying for your daughter's surgery this week. How did it go?").

Herman Horne, in *Jesus the Master Teacher*, says, "Jesus came not to answer questions, but to ask them; not to settle peoples' souls, but to provoke them." Jesus knew how to ask good questions at the right time to get people to think in new and deeper ways. Asking good questions is an excellent way of opening up disciple-making possibilities.

Skill #3 - Focusing

Imagine that you've had a very sore wrist for a couple of months and have finally set up an appointment with your doctor. Your doctor wants to hear the symptoms, but ultimately wants to discover and treat the underlying issue.

The focusing skill involves asking good questions (and sometimes offering advice) that helps the individual pinpoint the core issue. This sometimes takes a while. After identifying the main issue, I like to ask the person for 2-3 SMART action steps (specific, measurable, achievable, realistic, and time-bound) that will help them make progress in addressing the key issue. I will follow-up with them on these action steps, as I find that support and accountability are huge motivators. Even baby steps can create momentum that will help the individual continue to deal with the current situation (and others, as well).

Abraham Lincoln once said, "A goal properly set is halfway reached." As we help people set goals that they want to achieve, they will know where they need to go and feel empowered to move in that direction.

Skill #4 - Empowering

The final skill of empowering focuses on encouraging, affirming, celebrating and praying for the other person. We all need cheerleaders in our lives who spur us on.

I remember my second-grade teacher asking me if I would be willing to teach the other kids how to tell time. Now, you need to realize that, for most kids that age, their teacher and God are almost on the same level. Here was someone I deeply admired saying that I could teach others. She believed in me! Is it any wonder that public speaking and teaching have been a huge part of my life?

I love how Mo Cheeks, former NBA basketball

coach, did this with Natalie Gilbert. Natalie, a 13-year-old, had won a contest to sing the national anthem at an NBA game. But when the time came, she faltered partway through and didn't know what to do. Cheeks came alongside, put his arm around her and said, "It's all right." He proceeded to sing along with her for a while. With Cheek's encouragement, Natalie's confidence returned and she finished the song.

All of us can come alongside others – to give them the strength to carry on.

Every conversation has the potential to become some-thing more than a social interaction. As we listen well, ask good questions that open up new possibilities, focus the conversation on key issues, and empower the person to take next steps, we will make disciples.

Structured Coaching Conversations

Coaching really is a way of life as we seek to interact in disciple-making ways. However, there is also a place for using these four skills in structured coaching sessions where we intentionally engage in disciple-making conversations during several planned sessions.

In this section, I will describe the five stages of a structured coaching conversation using the *COACH Model for Christian Leaders* by Keith Webb. The five stages correspond to the letters in the word COACH: 1) Connect, 2) Outcome, 3) Awareness, 4) Course, and 5) Highlights.

Connect – Build Rapport and Trust

Every coaching conversation requires a meaningful

connection so that the other person is willing to share and explore possibilities. At the start of the session, it's important to take time to build rapport, revisit goals from the previous session, and pray together.

Here are some sample connecting questions:

1. How have you been?
2. What progress have you made on the action steps you identified last time?

You will notice with the last question that the focus is on progress; not whether they fully achieved the action steps. It's important to celebrate baby steps in the right direction. Even small steps can contribute to forward momentum for taking more and even bigger steps down the road. "The longest journey begins with a single step" (Steve McIlwain).

Outcome – Find out What the Person Would Like to Discuss

In a coaching session, it is highly beneficial for the coachee to identify an outcome for the conversation. This helps focus the interaction on what's most important to them, leading to better results. Asking good questions can probe beneath the surface of a presenting issue and uncover something that might be even more critical to discuss. Make sure that the outcome is achievable during the time you have together.

Here are a couple sample outcome questions:

1. What would be most helpful for us to work on?
2. What result would you like to take away from our conversation?

Awareness – Discover More about the Issues and Current Reality

One of the biggest benefits of coaching is that, when the coach asks good questions, it can expand awareness around key issues that the coachee may need to address. We want to ask good, open-ended questions that do not lead the person in the direction we think they should go. People are much more likely to own and act on something if they discover it themselves.

Here are some awareness questions:

1. What are the keys points in understanding this situation?
2. What other factors are influencing this situation?
3. How would you describe God's perspective on this situation?

The key in the awareness stage is to ask questions from multiple angles that help the coachee see the situation in different ways.

Course – Determine Next Steps

Many coaching conversations fail to challenge the coachee to act. The *COACH Model* gently pushes coachees to identify and follow through on two or three action steps that will help them address their key issues. The action steps should be SMART, so that coachees have a specific target and can sense whether they're making progress.

Here are three examples of course questions:

1. What options do you have?

2. Which of these options would you like to do?
3. How will you do them?

Highlights – Share Lessons and Goals

At the end of a coaching session, it's important to capture the key points and action steps emerging from the conversation. Don't summarize for them, but let them tell you their main takeaways. In fact, your key points may be different from theirs and we want them to run with the ideas they already own. Take time to pray for them and their action steps. This can be very encouraging and empowering.

Here are some highlights questions:

1. What would you like to remember from this time?
2. What parts of this discussion were particularly helpful?
3. What awareness do you have now that you didn't have before?

Coaching others in our everyday conversations and in structured coaching times is a highly effective way of making disciples in a personal, in-depth kind of way.

During my years as a pastor, church planter and missionary, I thoroughly enjoyed coming alongside people to help them take next steps in their discipleship journey. Looking back, I wish I had learned the COACH Model earlier; it has made a huge difference in my disciple-making effectiveness with my family, friends, other leaders, people in my church and students.

In the next chapter, we will wrap up the 11 essential elements of making disciples in the church by looking at the individual practice of spiritual disciplines.

Reflection/Discussion Questions

1. What do you make of your church's "Coaching and Mentoring" score on the Church Discipleship Assessment (see login information at the end of the book)?

2. What stands out to you from this chapter?

3. What do you already do in some of your conversations to turn them into disciple-making opportunities?

4. Take a moment to assess your use of the four skills (listening, asking good questions, focusing, and empowering) on a scale of 1-10.

    a. _____ Listening
    b. _____ Asking good questions
    c. _____ Focusing
    d. _____ Empowering

5. Which of the four skills would you like to grow this next month? How might you do so?

6. If you are discussing these questions as a group, I would invite you to break into partners. Think of a word that describes something about your life right now. Each person should take one minute to talk about his or her word choice and the reasons for choosing it. The other person should just listen for the entire minute. After both people have shared, the person who was listening should reflect back what they heard the other person say. Feel free to share the

content of the conversation, but also mention any struggles and longings you "heard" behind the words themselves.

7. After both people have shared what they heard, take some time to debrief. What was it like to have someone just listen to you for a full minute? As the person reflected back what they heard, how did you feel? What did you learn about yourself?

8. How might you turn the following close-ended questions into open-ended questions that invite dialogue?

    a. Are you happy about this decision?
    b. Is your supervisor in agreement with this?

9. Sometimes, our questions are actually leading questions that point people in the direction we think they should go. These are usually not very effective. How might you change the following leading questions into neutral questions?

    a. What part does your negative attitude play in this problem?
    b. Have you considered a student loan to finance your education?

10. Thinking about a more structured approach to coaching/mentoring, what has been your experience with coaching or mentoring (both as a coach/mentor and as someone being coached/mentored)?

11. What do you see as some of the advantages of a structured coaching conversation that occurs over several sessions? Disadvantages?

12. What would your church need to do to develop even more of a coaching/mentoring culture where people intentionally make disciples through both structured and unstructured coaching/mentoring?

13. What other thoughts do you have about coaching as an important ingredient in the disciple-making process?

Note: If you are interested in going through the official COACH training using Keith Webb's model (or hosting a COACH training event for your church), you can contact MinistryLift (www.ministrylift.ca). MinistryLift offers 1-day, 2-day, or 3-day versions of the training. We can also deliver a shorter introduction to the approach if that works better for your church.

Chapter 11
Spiritual Disciplines

Even as I focus on spiritual disciplines in this chapter, I'm keenly aware that God often uses challenges and opportunities in our lives to stretch our faith. Nonetheless, I'm convinced that our spiritual practices like prayer and meditating on Scripture prepare us to handle and even make the most of those stretching experiences.

Over the centuries, Christians have used a tool called a "Rule of Life" to support their spiritual growth. A Rule of Life is an intentional plan to deepen our relationship with God and to receive more from Him (e.g. strength, wisdom) so that we can love Him more deeply and serve Him more effectively.

One Christmas, my brother-in-law gave all his siblings and their spouses a book called *Emotionally Healthy Spirituality* by Peter Scazzero. When I opened the present and saw the cover of the book, I wondered if perhaps he was trying to tell me something!

I actually found the book incredibly helpful in expanding my view on spiritual disciplines. In the book, Scazzero describes 12 spiritual disciplines that make up a Rule of Life. Some of them like play/recreation and emotional health are surprising additions to some of the classic practices like prayer and Bible study. As I read the book, I came to realize that all of life is an act of spiritual discipline. Engaging in spiritual disciplines help us to orient our entire lives toward God.

As I briefly explore the 12 spiritual disciplines in this chapter, I invite you to consider what you are doing in each of the areas and then prayerfully discern how God might have you strengthen some of them. At the end of the chapter, you will find a Rule of Life worksheet that you can use for this reflection exercise.

Scripture

How are you currently engaging with Scripture? Perhaps you attend a worship service at your church or participate in a small group Bible study. I have a Bible Reading Plan app on my phone that takes me through the Bible in a year (I tend to fall a bit behind). Some have found that life journaling is an effective way of capturing what God is saying through a passage. We want to engage with Scripture in such a way that we hear from God and remember (and apply) what He has said throughout the day.

Silence and Solitude

Judy Brown has said, "What makes a fire burn is space between the logs, a breathing space." Silence and solitude can create these breathing spaces, which allow us to listen to God, discern His leading, and respond wisely and courageously. Jesus, himself, often went off by himself to spend intimate time with his Heavenly Father.

I try to insert silence into my daily routines (e.g.

sometimes driving to work in silence). Taking prayer walks in the morning gives me time for quiet reflection. I also like to go on extended prayer retreats of several hours or even a day or two.

After my last daylong prayer retreat, I came away refreshed, more in love with Jesus and with a keener sense of His priorities for my life. Silence and solitude provided the space that I needed for God to do a deeper work in my life.

Prayer

Increasingly, I want to develop a lifestyle of prayer where I naturally worship, give thanks, and petition God throughout the day. Setting aside time for prayer each day helps move me in that direction. For example, my morning prayer walks are a great way to spend time alone with God. I also periodically embark on longer prayer retreats, as I mentioned under "Silence and Solitude."

Study

This Rule of Life element refers to intentional study of a particular topic. Lifelong learning is so important for helping us grow in our capacity to serve God more effectively.

Sabbath

Mark Buchanan in his book, *The Rest of God*, says we experience Sabbath when we stop doing what is necessary and do that which gives life. What gives you life? How are you currently taking time to focus on God and to replenish your body, mind and spirit? Reggie McNeal reminds us that "Putting off Sabbath means putting off life."

Simplicity

We live in an age of distractions. Objects and activities threaten to clutter and overwhelm our lives. Living simply involves removing distractions and unnecessary attachments so that we can focus more fully on God and live out His calling on our lives.

Play and Recreation

When I first read *Emotionally Healthy Spirituality*, I was a little shocked that play and recreation made it onto Scazzero's list of spiritual disciplines. Yet, the more I thought about it, the more I realized that these activities are absolutely essential for our wellbeing. True recreation leads to the "re-creation" of our bodies, minds, and spirits, which allows us to worship God more deeply and serve Him more effectively.

Service and Mission

We know from Scripture that we have been created in Christ Jesus for good works, which God prepared beforehand (Eph. 2:10). This passage indicates that God has a special plan for each of us. Identifying and obeying God's call contributes to a fulfilling and fruitful ministry. How are you living out God's call on your life in practical ways?

Care for the Physical Body

As we take good care of our bodies as an act of worship to God, we will be in a better physical state to attend to and live out God's call. In one of the courses I teach at MB Seminary, I ask students to track their eating and exercise patterns for a month using an app like the MyFitnessPal Calorie Counter. The goal of the activity is to promote awareness of how our diet and physical activities impact our overall health.

Emotional Health

Emotional intelligence (EI) is a hot topic these days. The basic premise of EI is that, as we become increasingly self-aware, we will be able to better manage ourselves, notice what is going on in the people around us, and manage our relationships. We can increase our self-awareness by doing things like paying attention to our feelings, journaling about them, or discussing them with someone we trust. If you're interested in increasing your emotional intelligence, I highly recommend the *Emotional Intelligence 2.0* book and accompanying assessment.

Family

When I was starting out in pastoral ministry, one of my mentors gave me a book called *Man of Vision*. The book chronicles the life of Bob Pierce, founder of World Vision and the person who helped Samaritan's Purse get off the ground. In the book, Marilee Pierce Dunker, one of Pierce's daughters, describes a man deeply committed to God and His work with the poor and destitute around the world. Yet, somehow, Pierce lost sight of his family. He and his wife separated and one of Pierce's daughters committed suicide. Late in life, Pierce realized some of the errors of his ways and was reconciled with his wife. Sadly, it was too late to do so with his daughter.

Reading this triumphant and tragic story as a young man had a profound influence on my life and leadership. It made me poignantly aware that leadership starts with me and in the home.

Note: In addition to the *Man of Vision* book, you can also read an online Christianity Today article, *Imperfect Instrument*, about Bob Pierce's life (www.bit.ly/2hUka17).

Community

We need companions in the journey of life – people who will support us along the way (and whom we will support, too). Loving, Christ-centered communities provide a place where maximum discipleship can occur.

As I mentioned at the start, I encourage you to prayerfully consider what you are doing in each of the Rule of Life areas and how God might want you to strengthen them (the Reflection/Discussion section at the end of this chapter will help you do so). Of course, the Rule of Life is simply a means for growing our relationship with God and becoming more effective in serving Him. I appreciate how Richard Foster expresses this idea in his book, *Celebration of Discipline*:

A farmer is helpless to grow grain; all he can do is provide the right conditions for the growing of grain...This is the way it is with the spiritual disciplines - they are a way of sowing to the Spirit...By themselves the spiritual disciplines can do nothing; they can only get us to the place where something can be done.

Reflection/Discussion Questions – Rule of Life Worksheet

Part One – Identifying Your Current Rule of Life and How You Might Strengthen It

Go through the 12 areas of a Rule of Life. Write down what you are already doing and what you could add that would strengthen them. Be realistic. If you are not doing something in an area and don't think you should, that's fine. Feel free to add new areas to the list.

1. Scripture (Psalm 1:1-3) – Reading, studying, memorizing the Bible

    a. What are you currently doing in this area?

    b. How could you strengthen this area?

2. Silence/solitude (Mark 1:35) – Taking time by yourself

    a. What are you currently doing in this area?

    b. How could you strengthen this area?

3. Prayer (Luke 11:1-4) – These are times each day that you set apart to focus on God (e.g. prayer, silence, reading, etc.)

    a. What are you currently doing in this area?

    b. How could you strengthen this area?

Spiritual Disciplines

4. Study (2 Timothy 2:15) – Intentional times of reading and studying (not just the Bible either)

    a. What are you currently doing in this area?

    b. How could you strengthen this area?

5. Sabbath (Exodus 20:8) – Taking time each week to stop working and do those things which help us focus on God and to replenish our bodies, minds and spirits

    a. What are you currently doing in this area?

    b. How could you strengthen this area?

6. Simplicity (Hebrews 12:1-2) – Removal of distractions and unnecessary attachments

    a. What are you currently doing in this area?

    b. How could you strengthen this area?

7. Play/recreation (1 Corinthians 6:19-20) – Doing things that breathe life into you, that re-create your body, mind, and spirit

    a. What are you currently doing in this area?

    b. How could you strengthen this area?

8. Service/mission (Ephesians 2:10) – Living out God's call on your life in practical ways

    a. What are you currently doing in this area?

    b. How could you strengthen this area?

9. Care for the physical body (1 Corinthians 6:19-20) – Includes diet, exercise, sleep patterns, work habits, etc.

    a. What are you currently doing in this area?

    b. How could you strengthen this area?

10. Emotional health (1 Corinthians 6:19-20) – Paying attention to feelings, perhaps journaling about them, discussing them with a trusted friend or counselor

    a. What are you currently doing in this area?

    b. How could you strengthen this area?

11. Family (Ephesians 5:22-6:4) – How can you build into your family relationships as a single or married person?

    a. What are you currently doing in this area?

    b. How could you strengthen this area?

12. Community (Hebrews 10:24-25) – Building friendships with people

    a. What are you currently doing in this area?

    b. How could you strengthen this area?

Part Two – Prioritization of Rule of Life Areas

Choose two of the Rule of Life areas that you believe you need to focus on, so that you can draw closer to God and increasingly live out His call on your life. For each area, develop five action steps that are SMART (specific, measurable, achievable, relevant and time-bound):

1. Rule of Life Area #1 -

    a. SMART Action Step #1 –

    b. SMART Action Step #2 –

    c. SMART Action Step #3 –

    d. SMART Action Step #4 –

    e. SMART Action Step #5 –

2. Rule of Life Area #2 -

    a. SMART Action Step #1 –

    b. SMART Action Step #2 –

    c. SMART Action Step #3 –

    d. SMART Action Step #4 –

    e. SMART Action Step #5 –

Chapter 12

Next Steps

We've covered some important ground in the preceding chapters. I don't pretend to believe that the 11 disciple-making elements we've explored represent the final word on developing a disciple-making approach in your church. Yet, I think they do represent a good starting point.

Where do you go from here? If you're like me, you've seen many wonderful change initiatives start off strong only to be abandoned and forgotten after a few months or years. How can we implement change that lasts? In their book, *The 4 Disciplines of Execution*, McChesney, Covey and Huling describe a process that can help any church (or other organization) make change stick over the long haul. I want to show you how the process works with MinistryLift, the non-credit training arm of the MB Seminary, and suggest some ways that we can apply it to developing a disciple-making strategy in our churches.

Step #1 – Determine Your Wildly Important Goal(s) (WIGs)

"Don't ask 'What's most important?' Instead, begin

by asking, 'If every other area of our operation remained at its current level of performance, what is the one area where change would have the greatest impact?'" (p. 32).

With wildly important goals (WIGs), less is more. If you have 2-3 goals, you are likely to achieve all of them. If you have 4-10 goals, you will likely only achieve 1-2 of those goals. With 11-20 goals, you will probably achieve none of them.

In MinistryLift, our WIG this year is to increase participation by 50% in our five training ministries (live participation in training events, video views in our Resource library, blog views, and engagement via Facebook and Twitter). We believe that achieving this WIG will help us to achieve our mission – to build capacity in people to love God more deeply and serve Him more effectively.

As you think about developing a discipleship strategy in your church, what is the one area where change would have the greatest impact on your capacity to make growing disciples of Jesus? Develop a SMART (specific, measurable, achievable, realistic, time-bound) WIG that focuses on this area.

Let's say your church wanted to focus on coaching as your key growth area for developing a stronger disciple-making approach. One possible WIG would be to have 30 trained coaches involved in structured coaching relationships by the end of the year. Perhaps, you identify prayer as your key growth area. A prayer WIG could be to have 100 active users on your church's prayer app by the end of the year.

It may feel a little strange at first to set these kinds of disciple-making goals. Shouldn't it just happen naturally as God moves in people's lives? God definitely wants to transform lives; yet, He often chooses to do so through us and the processes we set up. Having a definitive WIG will help you stay on track with God's priorities for your church and not become distracted by other things.

Step #2 – Act on the Lead Measures

As we think about achieving WIGs, it's helpful to differentiate between lag and lead measures. Lag measures capture what has already happened. For example, with the MinistryLift WIG, we can look at data from the past to see how we're tracking in each of the five training ministries. Lag measures are important. Yet, if we want to accomplish our WIG, we need to be proactive and take steps that move those lag measures in the right direction. These steps are called lead measures.

Let's say that I decided to lose 10 pounds over the next two months. At the end of every day, I hop on the weigh scale to see how I'm doing. What I see on the weigh scale is a lag measure. Now, how do I actually make the weigh scale results line up with my WIG of losing 10 pounds? I need to implement lead measures like exercising 30 minutes each day or eating smaller meal portions.

Two years ago, our lead measure at MinistryLift was promotional touches. We wanted to get the word out about MinistryLift through social media, personal conversations, presentations, and numerous other means. Every month, we set a goal for how many promo touches we wanted to do. It was exciting to see how this kind of lead measure drove us toward accomplishing our WIG.

Thinking about the coaching WIG example in the previous step, what kind of lead goal would motivate the person or team responsible for the WIG to make it happen? One lead measure could be personally contacting people about becoming a coach. To make it even more definite, we could set a lead measure goal of inviting five people per month to consider becoming coaches.

With the prayer app WIG, we could use a promo touch kind of lead measure. Because the commitment level is less than becoming a coach, we could combine personal invitations with more general promo touches like emails and worship service announcements. What we did with MinistryLift promo touches is we weighted the various approaches differently (e.g. sharing the vision with a small group carried more weight than a quick conversation with an individual). A possible lead measure target would be to do 20 promo touches per month.

What kind of lead measure will help you accomplish your WIG? Developing a strong lead measure is a proactive step that will help you focus your energies in the most productive direction.

Step #3 – Keep a Compelling Scoreboard

"People are most satisfied with their jobs (and therefore most motivated) when those jobs give them the opportunity to experience achievement" (*The 4 Disciplines of* Execution, pp. 75-76). A scoreboard helps team members see how they're doing. They can celebrate successes and reach deeper to address performance gaps when necessary.

In MinistryLift, we started off slow with achieving our WIG two years ago. Yet, as we persisted with our promo touch lead measure, we began to see the scoreboard change (we used a simple line graph that showed both our target and actual numbers). Seven months into the process, we finally caught up to where we needed to be with our lag measure. Two months later, we had surpassed our participation goal for the entire year!

As you think about a scoreboard, you will want to have something that shows both your lag and lead measures. Using the coaching example, you would want a scoreboard that shows the number of trained coaches who are coaching others (lag measure) and the number of personal invites extended to people to become coaches (lead measure). With the prayer app WIG, your lag measure would be the number of active users. Your lead measure would be the number of promo touches.

Step #4 – Create a Rhythm of Accountability

How do you stay focused on your WIG and the lead measures that move you towards accomplishing your WIG? This is where many teams fall short. Consequently, team members lose interest in the initiative and the initiative loses momentum. According to McChesney et al., "Unless we consistently hold each other accountable, the goal naturally disintegrates in the whirlwind [of daily activities]" (p. 13).

Each week, the MinistryLift team takes 20-30 minutes to hold each other accountable for producing results. Each of us identifies 1-3 specific action steps related to the lead measure that we will do over the next week. The following week, we report on our progress and identify new action steps. This accountability forces us to stay focused on accomplishing what we have identified as the most important goal for our ministry.

What kind of accountability rhythm would work best in your context with the discipleship WIG you have in mind? Without some sort of regular accountability time that includes backward checking and forward planning, most new initiatives will falter and fail over time.

The four disciplines of execution provide a process for helping any ministry team accomplish God's plan for their ministry. When it comes to strengthening your church's discipleship approach, the stakes are huge. Make sure that you invest the necessary time and effort to position your church for maximum discipleship. You won't regret it!

Reflection/Discussion Questions

As a wrap-up to this book, you will have the opportunity to set out an action plan for strengthening your church's discipleship approach by using the *The 4 Disciplines of Execution* as a planning framework. For more information on the four disciplines, I highly recommend reading the book. You can also watch an excellent video overview on YouTube (www.bit.ly/2yEJqfK). Watching this 20-minute overview of the approach would be a good lead-in to the following discussion.

1. Step #1 - As you think about developing a discipleship strategy in your church, what is the one area where change would have the greatest impact on your capacity to make growing disciples of Jesus? Develop a SMART (specific, measurable, achievable, realistic, time-bound) WIG (wildly important goal) that focuses on this area.

2. Step #2 - What kind of lead measure will help you accomplish your WIG?

3. Step #3 - What kind of scoreboard (that captures both lag and lead measures) will motivate you and your team to reach further and press harder to accomplish your WIG?

4. Step #4 - What kind of accountability rhythm would work best in your context with the discipleship WIG you have in mind?

5. As you think about your responses to the previous four questions, what challenges do you anticipate? How will you try to overcome these challenges?

May the Lord give you much strength and wisdom as you seek to make disciples in a maximum way in and through your church!

Access to the Church Discipleship Assessment

As a part of purchasing this book, you have free access to the Church Discipleship Assessment at www.MinistryLift.ca/church-discipleship-assessment.
Login – CDA
Password – Maximum Discipleship

Made in the USA
Lexington, KY
05 December 2019